Printed by M.J. Albert in the United States
of America.

First printing, 2021.

ISBN 9798485604868

M.J. Albert Books

3527 S Federal Way Ste 103 #1008

Boise ID 83703

www.mjalbertbooks.com

Introduction

In 2019 I was a long-distance truck driver and was making great money. I saved even more money because since I was single and my kids were all grown, I didn't need to rent or own a residence. I basically lived in my truck and I'd go visit my kids or stay in a motel for a few days when I took time off.

Life was okay. I always loved being on the road so making my living out there was a dream come true for a while. One perk was being able to listen to audio-books. I've always loved stories from as far back as I can remember. As I drove each day, I'd blue tooth my Audible Phone App into the truck's sound system and listen to a book. Over the course of nine years I amassed an audio library of over 700 titles.

Then one day I had a dentist appointment. For some reason, I passed out in the dentist chair. I've been going to the dentist for more than fifty years and, though it wasn't my favorite thing to do, I had never fainted or passed out before.

When I came to, there were paramedics ready to take me to the hospital and I was told I'd had a seizure. I'd never had any type of seizure before in my life, and I suspect this wasn't a brain malady but exhaustion. I'd pushed myself from Sunday night to Wednesday morning in order to get from Cleveland OH to Dallas TX and make a 6 am appointment to unload. Once I got to Dallas, I needed a maintenance check and oil change for my truck. Having my truck in the shop meant I had nowhere to sleep, so when I got the truck back from the shop Wednesday night, I'd been awake nearly 24 hours. I went to the dentist the next morning on about six hours of sleep and, I think, just passed out in the chair. But I was referred to a neurologist who made the call that I was no longer going to be able to drive commercially.

Luckily, I had purchased disability insurance and so I was set for a year. I looked around for something else to do and came across an expert who marketed books. She was putting together a group of students who she was going to train in her marketing strategy. I signed on and loved helping authors market their books ever since.

I've helped authors achieve Amazon Best Seller status for their books for a couple years now. I haven't missed once; I'm batting a thousand if you don't mind the baseball metaphor.

But I've noticed that achieving Amazon Best Seller status is not going to instantly make an independent author able to quit their day job just off the royalties. It's a great start, and a way of learning book marketing but just by itself it's not all that helpful. You can put it as an accolade on your website or author page, but today it's not even all that uncommon.

I have studied and read book marketing since learning this skill, and I can say that for the successful Independent Author, writing is only about 40% of the job. To be successful, you have to be marketing yourself and your books. You must also do your best to stay ahead of the curve, as things change in this business a lot. Almost weekly some new idea or strategy is touted. Some new company claims to be able to turn you into a success.

My hope is that with this book, I give you the foundation for success in your marketing. Whether you plan to write as a career or have written a book you hope will bring you clients for your business, marketing is important and should be taken every bit as seriously as your writing.

Here's to your success and lucrative career as an independent book author!

M.J. Albert September 2021

You can contact me at my website https://www.mjalbertbooks.com/contact-me.html

Or email me: mj@mjalbertbooks.com

The Audience

Before we get started, try to think a little bit about who you are writing for. Who are the people who are going to buy your book? What are they reading now? What authors do they prefer?

You'll want to know who your audience is so that you can target them as your market. Before even beginning to learn about marketing your book you have to have that clearly in mind, otherwise you'll just be flailing about hoping for your audience to find you among the millions upon millions of books available.

So, start with this question: What are my readers reading? A good exercise for finding this out is to open up Amazon, and type in the genre or topic you have written in. For instance, if you write contemporary romance novels, or 'RomCom', type in contemporary romance into the Amazon search box. Look at the books Amazon is showing you. Read their book descriptions.

When you find a book your audience is most likely buying, note it down with the author, title of the book, and the ASIN.

Another great exercise is to visit a bookstore. Notice how books are categorized in your local Barnes & Noble or other bookstore. Take note of the major genres offered, look at what books are in that section, and find the section where your book fits. If you can't find one, you may be in trouble. Book stores have limited space available and so stock only popular categories. If you can't find the category your book fits in, chances are it's not a popular one and you will have trouble marketing your book.

Read the genre you are writing for. The only way to write what your market will want to buy is to know what the tropes of that market are. You can write for yourself, and still be successful but you will spend a lot of time and effort finding your audience. If you don't see where your book fits, start with envisioning your audience, figure out what sort of books that audience loves to read, and target those authors, read them, look at their sales pages. If you find your book isn't appealing to that particular market, try something different. Look for other genres / topics where your book might fit in.

The more I learn about book marketing the more I discover that we are not in competition with each other so much as we are lumped together into genres or groups. If you try and stand outside this arrangement you are going to have a tough go at selling your work.

Now, on to the details!

Step 1 – A Professional Cover

Your book's cover is the front person for your book, the 'barker' of olden days when carnivals traveled between towns and men stood outside tents exhorting the crowd to come take a look. It's got to catch the eye of the reader, it must look professionally done, and it needs to convey the type of book you've written, genre for fiction or category for non-fiction. The difference in interest you will receive with a great design vs a mediocre one is huge.

The Five Elements of a Great Cover

1. **Title:** The title of your book is important in several ways.
   Your title should convey the hook of your story. It could be a keyword, but this is not necessary. Book Titles are indexed, but if you use it as a keyword then you aren't increasing your chances of ranking by having it in your title. (more on keywords later)
   Your title should indicate fiction genre / nonfiction category or at least help the book's cover point to the genre/type of work it is. The font used needs to fit the genre but can also be used to make the book stand out, normally in partnership with your artwork.

   When you choose a title, check it out on Amazon. Just go to the Amazon search box, type in the title you are thinking of using and make a note of what Amazon shows you. If most of the titles that come up are close to the title you are thinking of using, you might want to consider something different as you are going to have a lot of competition. The unspoken rule being that the closer to the top of a search page your book appears, the more likely someone is going to click on it and check out your sales page.

Use a font that will make the title stand out even when the book is viewed in thumbnail form.

2. **Subtitle**: A subtitle should be used to convey the genre or area of expertise of the author (if non-fiction). It can also be used to denote a particular sequence in a series. Some authors will even use two subtitles, one for genre / expertise, the other for validating the author or denoting the particular sequence of the book in a series. Subtitles can also contain keywords, but just note that if you put a keyword here, don't duplicate it when you set up the keywords for your published work. You don't get 'double credit' for using a

keyword in your title/subtitle and in your keyword list.

3. **The Artwork:** The visual needs to be eye catching. You want it to tell the reader what the genre/topic is, and you want it to stand out in a collection of similar books. It has to be professional looking, or most readers are going to ignore it. It should try to contain the hook of your story, but don't crowd a bunch of images on the cover to achieve this. The reader is going to make a split-second decision about checking your book out, and if there is too much going on, if the cover is too busy, they may just move on to the next cover. Keep it to no more than three separate images, and preferably just one major one. Don't choose artwork that comes from a single part of the book. If the art has to be explained by reading the book, you have it backwards. The art needs to explain the book, not vice versa.

4. **The Background:** Use the background artwork and/or color to enhance and complement the foreground artwork. It should say something about the ambiance

of your story as well as highlighting your artwork. You can use images in the background, but again keep them to a minimum and don't make your cover too complicated.

5. **Author Name:** This can be simple, just your pen name. Make it legible, some authors put it at the top of the book, some at the bottom, it really depends on the arrangement and where the eye is drawn when first looking at the book. If you aren't a name author with a large following, you don't want your potential reader's eye drawn immediately to your name, you want the focus to be on the artwork and/or title and subtitle. You can use an honorific or if you have won an award, make that part of your author name if you want. Some people suggest not doing that, it might look tacky, I think it's a personal choice and, even if it doesn't help, I don't think it will hurt your book's chances of being selected by a buyer.

The Five Purposes of a book cover

1. **It shows your book fits in:** If you look at book covers for a particular genre or even subgenre, you should be able to spot some similarities. Make sure your cover fits in to a selection of books targeting your readers.
2. **It stands out:** When looking at a selection of books your readers are interested in, your book needs to catch their eye. It needs to look professional and have enough sizzle that they are drawn to your cover and will click to find out more.
3. **Tone:** You want your readers to get a sense of the tone of your work. Is it light and humorous? Dark and suspenseful? If the cover is confusing, many people are going to skip over it.
4. **Credibility:** Possibly more important for non-fiction where people are reading to be informed or taught something. It could be an honorific on your name, a badge for

bestseller status or an award, or simply denote the type of book you have written. You want your cover to convey that you are a competent storyteller worth reading.

5. **Category / Genre:** Make sure your readers will know that this book is one of a particular type they love to read. **You want to be clear as to the genre /sub-genre/topic your book fits into.**

Where to get your cover designed

(note: I have no financial stake in, or received compensation from any of these companies)

1. **High end professionals**: If you can afford a budget of $500 to $1,000 I highly recommend you seek out an experienced professional such as these:

a. DamonZa This company has been doing covers for quite some time and their artists are very experienced, and you will get a

professional sizzling cover from them.
https://damonza.com/

b. eBookLaunch: Another very experienced, professional company that does other things such as editing, formatting, ad design, and book covers. They do wonderful work, and you can buy a package deal from them if you are looking for things other than just the cover design. https://ebooklaunch.com/book-cover-design/

c. Reedsy: Reedsy is a place where professionals can offer their services and bid on jobs offered by clients. They have a variety of offerings from editing, coaching, ghostwriting, website design, marketing, etc. You can upload your book or even write it in Reedsy, then choose the service you want and choose up to five professionals that you think would be a good fit and get their bids on your project. In order to be considered for Reedsy, a professional must meet high minimum standards. You can check out a designer's work on the site so you get an idea of what sort of covers they have created in the past.

You can expect experienced cover designers to give you an offer close to what Damonza or EbookLaunch will quote. Reedsy charges a service fee on top of the designer's bid. https://reedsy.com/

2. Mid- priced professionals – These sites have professional cover designers, some of varying experience, that offer cover design at a lesser rate than the ones I designated as high-end pros.

a. **100Covers**: You choose a package, currently they run $100, $200, or $300 and you fill out a form that asks for details about your work, what you are expecting, etc. A project manager will contact you and you will work with them. They in turn, work with the artist to design your cover and/or other book related art depending on what package you choose. One feature you get with 100Covers is a 50% discount on the next book if they are in a series. I've used them and am very happy with the result.

b. **Fiverr.com**: This site is similar to Reedsy, but has less requirements for their professionals. If you use this site you could get a cover done for as little as $30. However, you need to really look at the portfolio of the designer and get a good sense of what sort of covers they are designing and whether or not they might be able to turn your vision into a great cover for your book. I wouldn't recommend using artists here unless you really know what you want and can be precise in your instructions. Fiverr is an international site and many artists in third world countries use it. This isn't a bad thing, I've worked with some professional artists there and Fiverr is protective of their reputation, but many artists do not understand English as well as a native speaker. Just be ready to spend a lot of time going back and forth with designers from this site. Also, I don't like the way Fiverr is set up. I've used it enough times that I have several completed projects there, but it's not easy to go back and find one particular project.

3. D-I-Y – Many authors choose to do their own covers, and this can result in a great design if you know what you are doing,

however many experts say it's not a good idea for the same reason it's not a good idea for a lawyer to represent herself in court. There are classes you can take in design that not only give you a great cover for your book but give you a way of earning extra income if you learn enough to create covers for other authors.

a. **PhotoShop**: This is the premier software used by most professional graphic designers. It offers unlimited potential in creating stunning graphics. However, it's got a steep learning curve and not everyone has the time, patience, and/or inclination to learn it. Plus, the price is expensive. If you do learn to use it proficiently however, you could design sizzling covers and even become a professional designer.
https://photoshop.com/en

b. **Canva**: This is a web based graphic design program that you pay a monthly subscription to use. It has tons of graphics, fonts, readymade title fonts, pictures, templates, etc. available and it's user friendly. I designed two decent covers in about an hour the first time I used it. They weren't up to the standards of a PhotoShop design, but they met the basic five elements / five purposes a cover should deliver. The price is very reasonable, about $13 a month and the first 30 days are free. A neat feature is the team collaborative aspect. You can work on a design with a team of people, designate who is responsible for what, and finish a design in real time together. https://www.canva.com/

c. GIMP: This is freeware, in other words open-source programming. GIMP stands for Gnu Image Manipulation Program. I've never tried it, but it appears to be on the same level with PhotoShop in terms of the images you can design with it. Worth trying if you think you can design your own covers! https://www.gimp.org/

Common publishing dimensions

For ebooks, Amazon requires covers to be a minimum 2560 x 1600 pixels and have a ratio of 1.6:1.

Paperbacks can be one of several different dimensions, the most popular are 5x8 or 6x9. The cover, spine, and back cover total dimensions will be determined by a number of factors such as the number of pages, the font used, and the paper style selected. Kindle Direct Publishing does have an excel spreadsheet with sizing measurements an author can use to create a paperback cover.

Audio book covers are typically 3200 x 3200 pixels and 1:1 ratio (square).

For more information:

My Blog post on cover design:

https://www.mjalbertbooks.com/independent-marketing/six-steps-to-best-seller-book-marketing-presents7611654

An interesting experiment using ten Fiverr cover designers.
https://m.youtube.com/watch?v=7__-AhQE4WY&feature=youtu.be&fbclid=IwAR3hAmAAvSb57MZoIqvsa3MWTNVHwNCC7WiXqENNodoCh9MtyU-UWO_P9kw

Step 2 – Book Description (Sales Copy)

How do you go about looking for the next book you want to buy? You might look for a new book by one of your favorite authors. You may be looking for a bargain, a new author in your favorite genre or for a specific topic.

So, unless you have a specific author or book in mind, you will browse by keyword, genre, or category. What appears when you search like this, is a bunch of covers and book titles. You will click on the one that grabs your attention first, hoping to learn more. You'll base your purchase decision on what catches your interest: how successful the book is, the expertise of the author, reader reviews, or the book description (sales copy).

This is the blurb you find on the back cover of most paperbacks and hardbound books. In the digital world, it is the description you see once you click on a book cover. Once a potential buyer has seen your cover and decided it's worth finding out more, they will either decide to buy, save it for later, or skip over and find another book. Their decision will be based mostly on your cover and book description (sales copy).

This makes the sales copy the second most important marketing tool, because to get to it, the book's cover must draw in the buyer. Cover first, sales copy second. It's the deciding factor, and if you don't get it right, you will lose sales. If you are not getting many conversions (people who clicked on your book and 'converted' to buyers) most likely you need to improve your sales copy.

Because we are writers, we have the tendency to think we can write anything. *I wrote the book, I'm the expert, and I will do the best job of writing the description.* This is true up to a point, but writing sales copy requires different skills than writing a book or even a short story. You can learn to do sales copy, with practice. In this book

I will show you how to write sizzling sales copy that will get people to click the 'buy' button.

As an author, I never gave much thought to writing the description. It's just that summary on the back cover after all. A couple paragraphs, no big deal, right? That could not be more wrong. I found out that in marketing a book the small blurb is what closes the deal for you with potential buyers. The cover gets them there, the sales copy is your closer.

So, how do you write a description that will work? We are writers and most of us tend to think because we have mastered the art of writing a novel, a short little blurb to describe our book is going to be easy. I mean, I just wrote 100,000 words worth of a great story, I can write a couple paragraphs telling people what the book is about!

This is a mistake however. That two paragraphs is going to be essential to the number of people who will read your 100,000 word novel. It needs to be taken seriously. You could hire a professional like me to do it for you, (shameless promo) but if you follow a few simple rules, it can be done by any writer, I think.

Step 1: Know your audience. Who do you envision buying your book? This has to do with genre, knowledge, or area of expertise. Did you write an epic fantasy? Then you want readers who enjoy that genre. Did you write a book on home repair? You are targeting do-it-yourselfers and new homeowners maybe.

Sit down and write out who you see buying your book. Have this audience firmly in mind as you write out ideas for your sales copy. Know the language these readers are familiar with.

Step 2: Capture your book's essence. Write out the theme of your book. Don't worry about making it short at this point, concentrate on getting the idea down on paper. You want the heart of your story.

Step 3: Include the major character(s) in your work (if fiction). Readers love good characters. People they would like to fall in love with, have a beer with, or people they would like to beat to a pulp, see go to jail, etc. But don't overdo it. Stick to the essential characters; the good, the bad, and maybe the sidekick.

If this is non-fiction biography, then you include the major person(s) you have written about and why this book is the one about that person that you should read.

For non-fiction expertise, write out the problem you are solving and talk about yourself; what makes you the expert to solve that problem.

Step 4: For Fiction, write out what the story is going to feel like. What emotions are you going to invoke in the reader as they devour your story. For non-fiction be sure to give the buyer a vision of what it will feel like to have the expertise and/or knowledge you are about to impart to them.

Step 5: Once you have it all written out, read it out loud to see if there is anything you are missing. Make any changes you think are necessary then start to whittle it down. Use a thesaurus to find shorter phrases or even one word to convey each thought. Take out any characters that are not essential to the core of your story. Remove all the words that don't add value or are not essential to your description. Keep doing this again and again until you can't cut anymore without losing the meaning of your story. Hopefully, you get it down to just a couple paragraphs.

Step 6: Write it again. Go through the same process but try some new angle. Remember to put a emotion into it. Do this until you have at least three and up to five different versions of your sales copy. You want each to entice the buyer into finding out what your story is, make them want to click that buy button or take the book to the sales desk in the bookstore. They just have to find out what happens in this book! Make it sizzle!

Now, email it to your friends and family. Hopefully you have a list of people who have agreed to give you an opinion and one day read your book and post a review for it. Ask this 'street team' to vote on which sales copy they like best. The one getting the most votes is the one you want to use.

DON'T BE AFRAID TO CHANGE IT! Some experts say that changing something on your novel will impact how Amazon presents your book, but I don't think it makes a major difference. If you are getting hits with your ads, but not many sales, one thing to look at is changing your book description. Make it sizzle! If you want an expert to write your blurb for you check out my website here: https://www.mjalbertbooks.com/blurb.html

Step 3 –Editorial and Reader Reviews

When a customer is looking for a book to buy, they stick with what they know. Authors they've read before or maybe one recommended to them. When the internet came along and shoppers were able to browse more books than ever before, this changed a bit. Vendors weren't limited by space to store the books anymore. Millions of electronic files could be stored with far less expense than thousands of actual books.

Customers still look for books by authors they are familiar with, but more and more readers seek out new authors. There are readers out there who search for new material, new writers, new stories. For most of us who write these stories, these are the people we want to get our books in front of. They are our customers and potential fans.

So how do you get customers to consider your book? I read somewhere that if you put every book published in a day in a row, you would have to travel at 90 mph to keep up with them! This means there are more books published in one minute than you will possibly read in a year. So, getting your book noticed would seem a daunting task. Thankfully, there is a system that does just that.

I have discussed the two main ways to attract customers: The book's cover and the book's description. But potential buyers also want to know they are not wasting their money on books that might turn out to be trash. No one likes the experience of buying a book that is badly written.

Before buying a book, we want to know that it's worth reading. This, of course, is sort of a "catch-22" situation. You can't really know if a book is worth buying without reading it and you can't read it without first buying it! So, what to do?

We look to see who has read the book and given their opinion of it. We look for reviews.

Reviews are perhaps one of the most difficult parts of an independent author's business. You need people to read your book(s) before they can review, but you need reviews in order to get people to read your books. So how to break out of this cycle?

First you will need an Advance Review Copy (ARC) of your book. This should be edited but doesn't have to be completely polished or formatted yet. You can create an ARC simply by converting your manuscript into a pdf file. If you want to be a little more professional, you can find services that will convert your manuscript into an ebook version, like Calibre https://calibre-ebook.com/ Bookbaby https://www.bookbaby.com/ or Bookfunnel https://bookfunnel.com/. There are several ways you can get people to read and review your book but first a word of caution here. As most of your sales are most likely going to come through Amazon, you need to be aware that Amazon is very protective of their review process. They monitor it and are not at all forgiving when it comes to someone trying to skirt the system.

Which makes sense, Amazon wants their customers to have a great experience and if they read a bunch of fake reviews, make a purchase, and find out the product isn't what they expected, then customers will be unhappy and go buy elsewhere. (Assuming they can find somewhere else besides Amazon to buy!)

So, there are a few rules you need to know about Amazon reviews. **First,** an account must have purchased at least $50 worth of stuff from Amazon in order to be eligible to review a product. This is to ensure people aren't just creating a bunch of accounts in order to leave reviews.

Second, you cannot pay for an Amazon reader review. Let me be clear here, you CAN pay for an editorial review which you post using your Amazon Author account. You CAN'T pay for a reader review which has to be posted by the Amazon Customer. You can offer a free copy of your book, and ask for an honest review, but you absolutely cannot give the reviewer any incentive like a giveaway, gift certificate, raffle entry or anything of value in exchange for their review.

Editorial Reviews – These are reviews from influencers, other authors, publishers, or experts. You control these as they are entered through your Amazon Author Profile account. Getting them can be tricky. If you know someone who has pull in the genre or area of expertise you are writing in, then ask them for a review. Get the word out to family and friends that you've written a book and need some editorial (expert) opinions or reviews on it.

If you live near a University, you could consider contacting someone in the department that would coincide with what area you've written in. Preferences vary, but you might get lucky and find a professor willing to read your work and give you a review.

There are services that will review your work for a fee. These are editorial reviews so aren't subject to the reader review scrutiny that Amazon has in place. Since you control them, you are able to post or not post these reviews in their entirety or quotes from them.

Look for podcasts about your book's topic or genre.

Online Book Club - https://onlinebookclub.org/review-requests/

This service is pricey, but they will find an expert to review your work.

Kirkus Review - https://www.kirkusreviews.com/indie-reviews/

Another service that will review your work and give you an editorial review. It is also pricey, costing over $400 for a review.

There are other services out there, you can google them if you want. I only have given you these two as an example and because I know they are legit. You'll pay for the privilege, but they will deliver a review you can use on your website or as an editorial review on Amazon.

Reader Reviews:

There are services that you can pay for to get names and email addresses of people who have read and reviewed the same type of book that you've written. The goal is to have ten reviews before launching your first advertising campaign. Typically, only one in four people who say they will review your book actually will. So, our goal is to find forty people to commit to leaving a reader review.

Book Review Targeter

Owner: Debbie Drum

Website: https://debbiedrum.lpages.co/brt-new2-2019/

Cost: Basic membership is $19.95 per month. A pro subscription allows you to download more reviewer names for $37.95 per month and also includes a web crawler that will try to find the subscriber's email address.

Book Review Targeter or BRT, will search reviews for any book you enter into the website's application. It returns any Amazon account it finds that left a review for the book along with any contact info it finds. I've used BRT many times for clients and it works. The trick is to find books that you believe your readers would buy and that have more than 100 reviews. Fewer than that, and you risk the software not finding enough reviewers to contact. Of course, I have often had to run the app multiple times with different books in order to get a sizeable list. I generally shoot for over 100 names. BRT gives you the account name, website, and social media info. It all depends on what the reviewer has entered. Amazon, unfortunately, no longer allows account holders to enter an email address.

Positives: You get all the information you need to make a personal request to the reviewer to read your book. The book that is reviewed, a link to the reviewer's Amazon account page, a link to the book, how many stars, and a copy of the review itself. You can download the info into a csv file which can be opened by Excel or other spreadsheet program.

Negatives: This process is very time consuming. Many of the reviews are going to be dated and often so will the contact info. It's a good idea to try to choose newer books that have been published in the last year or so. I've signed up for the 'Pro' service on BRT and while it gives me a lot more reviewers, it's claim to finding email addresses has not proved to be very useful. I normally spend 8 to 10 hours generating a verified list of 50 people to contact. Overall I give it 3 stars

AMZ Discover

Owner:AMZ Discover Team

https://www.amzdiscover.com/

Cost: varies, one reviewer with contact info costs about 10 'coins'. Coins can be purchased initially in the amount of 900 for $9. So it costs 10 cents per interviewer, but you can purchase bulk amounts at a discount.

AMZ Discover is an easy-to-use website application. You paste in an Amazon URL (note: this isn't just for books, it can be used to find reviewers of any product sold on Amazon), and the software generates a list of reviewers for that product and tells you which ones have contact information. You can purchase the reviewers information for 10 coins (note: the software automatically prevents you from spending coins on reviewers who have no information).

Pros: AMZ returns good information and almost always attaches an email address to the reviewer. By entering multiple books that I think my client's readers would purchase, I can quickly generate a list of possible reviewers for any book. In less than 15 minutes I can have 50 to 100 possible reviewers to contact. I've used it on books I entered into BRT and it has come back with more names that were more usable (had email addresses).

Cons: The download mechanism seems to automatically download everything you've searched for. This means that if I've got three different books in three different genres loaded up in AMZ, I'm going to get all of that info in a csv file and then have to sort out the ones I am currently looking for. AMZ also only gives you the ASIN of the book, no title or author, I had to add those in. It also doesn't give you a copy of the actual review, if you want to see what that person wrote you have to go search it out. The cost is higher than with BRT because you pay by the name.

Overall though, I give AMZ 4 stars.

Pubby.co

This service allows authors to find readers who read the genre or area of interest you write in. You 'purchase' a book review with 'snaps'. To earn snaps you can buy them, review another author's book, invite someone to join Pubby, or use one of their author services.

I used it for a small book of mine and it worked. I got an Amazon review of 4 stars. It's worth looking into if you need reviews and either have time or money to spend getting them.

(Disclaimer: I am a member of Pubby, so if you use the link I do get credit for it)
Pubby.co

Advantage: You get the review posted on Amazon.

Disadvantage: It's going to cost you either time or money to get reviews this way.

I give Pubby 4 stars

BookSirens LLC.

Cost: varies but the main plan is $10 per ARC, and $2 for each download of your book.

I have only recently discovered this site. BookSirens offers the chance to get your book in front of a lot of readers. The way it works is you submit your book, if it is accepted you pay them $10 to offer your book as an ARC to their readers. Anytime one of their readers downloads your book, you are charged $2. (Note: If the same person downloads it more than once you are not charged more.) You tell them where you want the review posted (Goodreads or Amazon). You also control how many downloads you authorize. They also will convert your kdp file to a MOBI if you gift them your book.

They claim that about 75% of their readers who download a book actually review it. It seems expensive but it might be worth the cost to get reviews. Plus if the 75 percent number is true, it will save you a lot of time because with other methods the ratio is contacting 4 people to get 1 review. If their claim is correct, you would need 13 to 14 people to download your book in order to get 10 reviews at a cost of $38. ($10 for the book submitted and $2 per download). They also offer packages to authors for multiple books.

At this time, I don't have enough information to give a star rating to this service. When I've had more time to use them I will update this blog.

Online Book Club

Onlinebookclub.org/

Owner: Online book club LLCCost: There are different levels but the lowest priced review will run you $95.

I include this service only because I have used them to get editorial reviews. They currently do not offer any service to get reader reviews. The way it works is you submit your book and pay the fee. The service finds one of their reviewers to read and give a review. The review is posted on their site where you can copy and paste it as an editorial review or post a link to the review on their site.

My opinion is they charge way too much for what you get. I submitted a children's book I wrote and I got a review from someone. A member of onlinebookclub.org. She wasn't an authority, or a celebrity and I'm still confused as to why I was charged so much money for a basic review.

I give them 1 star

You can find templates for contacting potential reviewers in the supplement portion of this book. Before you contact them, it's a good idea to try and find out something about the reviewer so you can determine if they would be a good fit for your book.

Step 4 –Author Platform

Every author needs a way to interact with his/her readers. However, there are no hard and fast rules as to what form of interaction that should take. I think there are some basics you should be aware of but overall it's pretty much to you how you put yourself out there on an author website, book selling site, book review sites, genre fan sites, social media, or...?

I think every author should have a bio written up with a decent picture to go along with it. But even this isn't set in stone. If you write under several pen names maybe you don't want to use your self-portrait for each author bio.

Your biography should be short and simple. Readers like to know something about the author but again, there is no hard and fast rule as to what you write in your bio.

I think you should have one central landing page where readers can sign up for your mailing list/newsletter and this URL needs to be part of your book and your author profiles. While a website is not make or break for your career, at some point as you get more and more books written and find greater success, you will want one. A website is a place you control, unlike Bookbub, Amazon, Goodreads, etc. where you are creating an author page but it's all under the control of someone else ultimately. A website can be a place where you post news, upcoming events, future books, contests, etc. I would recommend you don't just throw a Wordpress site as they all tend to look the same and they appear not quite professional.

Building your email list

You can use a landing page and a reader magnet to draw potential readers to you and put them on your email list.

A reader magnet could be an excerpt from your book, a related short story or novella, even one book of a series.

It could also be something like a keychain or other cheap tchotchke. Optinmonster.com has a small book with 69 ideas for lead magnets. https://optinmonster.com/9-lead-magnets-to-increase-subscribers/.

A landing page is a website where your readers can sign up for your newsletter. A newsletter is important in order to get your readers involved and give them some reasons to read your work. You don't have to publish a newsletter every day or even every week, but you want to keep them thinking about you and your books.

There are several email services that can provide you with a landing page. I personally use mailerlite because they have the best versatility for a free account but there are others. I'm not going to reinvent the wheel, so go check out what has already been said here:

https://kindlepreneur.com/best-email-services-for-authors/

Bookfunnel is a website where you can upload your reader magnet and then use the site to draw potential fans and early readers in to sign up with your list. The site can be integrated with several different email services so as people grab your reader magnet and sign up for your list, they are automatically put on your mailing list.

Bookfunnel also has a great feature that allows you to combine forces with similar authors and join 'group' promotions where you all send out a link to each of your individual lists. I have joined a couple and did get a trickle of joiners every day, between 1 to 10 new signups with just a short story. It's well worth the effort.

https://bookfunnel.com/#we-deliver

Interacting with your readers is a personal choice kind of thing. Many authors will be comfortable with a Facebook account/group. Others may prefer not to be on social media at all. However you interact with your fans, you want to keep them engaged by regularly communicating with them.

Once you have published, sign up for BookBub, Amazon Author, and Goodreads to establish your author presence.

Bookbub

https://partners.bookbub.com/users/sign_up

Goodreads

https://www.goodreads.com/author/program

Amazon Author

https://author.amazon.com/

Step 5 – Categories and Keywords

This section is specifically going to talk about Amazon marketing. The same concepts may be true for other book services like Barnes & Noble or Apple Books, but let's face it, the King Kong of the book world is Amazon.

In previous sections you've learned how to make a great cover that draws the eyes of your readers. I've talked about writing sizzling sales copy to seal the deal when a reader clicks on your book. I have also talked about Editorial and Reader Reviews to give your potential buyers information on what others are saying about your book.

Now, I want to discuss how Amazon goes about bringing readers and books together. At least, part of the equation, which are the categories your book is placed in as well as the keywords people are using to search Amazon for a new book.

Keywords

Most of us, (if not all) are familiar with the rectangular white space on many websites that allows you to type in a word or a phrase and search their site for something specific. Someone wants to read a new horror novel. She types in 'Stephen King', 'scare me', or 'Horror' if she doesn't have a specific title in mind. Based on the keyword Amazon looks for popular books that its software associates with it.

This can happen in two ways, Amazon looks at the books authors/publishers have associated with that keyword when they set the book up. This is up to seven words or phrases and are subject to some rules, KDP Keywords. They also look at what books have these keywords set up in ad campaigns. The rules for these is far less strict and possibly more likely to put one book higher on the list then another.

What will definitely push a book up the list of possible selections is how popular the book is. Amazon uses a ranking for this called ABSR. Amazon Best Seller Rating. It's a ranking of total customer activity for the book and is updated hourly (though Amazon claims it could take 24 to 48 hours to update, which kind of boggles the mind). Anyway, how Amazon ranks book activity can be found here: Amazon Best Seller ranking.

So to get your book in front of people you will need to associate it with the right keywords. But how do you know which keywords will work? You could just guess and hope for the best. Maybe change them out every couple days and keep crossing your fingers you get it right. Even then, out of the seven that Amazon lets you associate with your book how can you

know which ones might be working and

which are not?

One way to do this is to clear your browser
history (so any keywords you have used
are not going to interfere) and go to
Amazon and start typing a keyword like
below :

If you have started with no history, then
Amazon is going to suggest keywords that
are currently popular. Copy them down
and try some more. This will work for ad

keywords where you can enter thousands of them if you wish, but how do you know they are your best choice for one of the magic seven you associate with your book?

I've only found one great way to do that. It's called Publisher Rocket and you can purchase it for $97 from Publisher Rocket. It's a great tool to have if you are going to market more than one book, and the price is very reasonable as it gives you so much more than the right keywords. If you are on a very limited budget and can't afford the $97, I will create a report for you with keyword and category recommendations. (see at the end).

Keywords have two important properties. First is their popularity. How many people are using that keyword is key (yah I went there). Second is the competition, in other words how many books are associated already with that keyword. The best ones to use will have lots of people using them but low in competition. Publisher Rocket will give you this information.

In Kindle Direct Publishing, each of the seven keywords you choose can have up to 50 characters. To maximize the number of indexing chances from Amazon, you should use some of the seven slots (I recommend three or four) to fill out the keyword slot as close to 50 characters as you can. Type in the best three (or four) keywords you get from Publisher Rocket by themselves in the first keyword slots. Then use more, putting a space between each word, to fill out 50 characters in each slot.

Her's a handy calculator you can use to keep your keywords to 50 characters. Just copy and paste into the KDP keyword window. Keyword Counter.

So to recap, use three of four of the keywords in KDP to hold the best keywords you found using Publisher

Rocket. Then create a string of other keywords, up to 50 characters each, for the remaining slots.

Feel free to write to me if you have questions! mj@mjalbertbooks.com

I will write more about keywords in the advertising section, but for those seven entries in your KDP account, the right keywords will make a very big difference.

Categories

Categories used in Amazon are different from the three codes you set up your book with in KDP. This is because the codes initially set are universal in nature, standard codes called BISAC (Book Industry Standards And Communication). These codes are used by the industry to categorize books into type and genre. When you first set up your book in KDP, you choose three of these.

What ones to choose is usually fairly obvious but using the link above you can find some recommendations so I'm not going to go into them much here. If you are going to sell your book 'wide' (both Amazon and other retailers) then they become more important.

Besides BISAC, Amazon uses its own categorization method that is basically a tree. The root of the tree starts at 'Any Department' and branches down into thousands of different categories. The ones we are concerned with here will be under 'books' or 'Kindle ebooks'.

Pick a book, type its name into the Amazon search window and click on it to find its sales page. Now scroll down until you see :

Product details

Publisher : Red Canoe Press (March 4, 2017)

Language : English

Paperback : 222 pages

ISBN-10 : 0995324204

ISBN-13 : 978-0995324206

Item Weight : 10.1 ounces

Dimensions : 5.5 x 0.56 x 8.5 inches

Best Sellers Rank: #44,754 in Books (See Top 100 in Books)
   #43 in Zen Spirituality
   #58 in Buddhist Rituals & Practice (Books)
   #75 in Holistic Medicine (Books)

Customer Reviews: ☆☆☆☆☆ ˅   645 ratings

Notice near the bottom are 3 rankings. These are categories this book is placed in, and where the book currently ranks in terms of activity. To get to the category tree. Click any one of those three. You will see something similar to this:

On the left you will see the category tree. Under the blue banner you'll see the current category you are looking in "Psychological Thrillers" in this case, and a list of the bestselling books in that category. Another way the Amazon software decides what books to show to potential buyers is the category and the book's ranking in that category. So if your book ranks #1 in this category, it is more likely to be shown to people searching for 'psychological thrillers' or other keywords associated with these types of books.

This means, if you can get your book to rank up in a category, Amazon is likely to show it to prospective buyers. But how to know which category to choose from?

First of all, please note that any category you choose must have at least 100 books in it for Amazon to recognize your status in that category. If you look at the books in the category, you will notice they are ranked from #1 through #50, with books ranked #51 to #100 available on a second page. What you want to do is find a category you have a good chance of ranking up in. Note the #1 book, but also record the ranking of the #10 book.

You want to find categories that are the lowest branch as possible as these tend to be the easiest to rank up in. However, you must be sure the category has at least 100 books in it. Any category with less than 100 is not considered for bestseller status and so won't be considered by the Amazon software based on category.

To do this, start at the top of the category tree for ebooks (you can do this with physical books but ebooks tend to sell better, and if offered, the paperback is always available as well). Now scroll until you find a major category that your book will fit in. You don't have to be too picky here, I've seen books in categories they don't really fit in like putting a fiction book on 18th Century London in a non-fiction English History category.

Amazon isn't real picky (with a few exceptions like foreign language or children's categories) about what category you choose. Many authors will go for the easiest category they can find to rank up in, whether their book fits that category or not. You can have your book in up to 10 categories. I suggest that if you can't find a category where reaching #1 can be done with an ABSR of 12,000 or so then choose at least one category that is maybe an almost fit for your book. Then use the additional categories as ones where your book fits in better.

Categories aren't used like keywords. People typically don't go searching by category. They will, however, click on a suggested book and follow that page. So categories are mainly internal. I would guess that it's possible you had no idea they even existed before reading this.

So here's what you need to do.

1. Find a category
2. Check to see that there are 100 books in it. (scroll down to the #50 book and click on 'page 2').
3. Determine the ABSR (Amazon Best Seller Rank) of the #1 and #10 book in that category and record them in a spreadsheet with category name, book title, ABSR, and category ranking.
4. Once you've found all the categories your book can possibly fit in, you want to determine the sales on the #1 and #10 book in each. You can do this with a free website. Amazon Sales Rank Calculator.
5. Record the sales of the #1 book and #10 book on your spreadsheet. This is your target. If you can beat the rankings with 12 to 15 books a day, I call that a keeper. But

either way you want to sort them by ranking and choose the easiest categories (assuming you are comfortable with putting your book in that category) to rank up in.

There is a much easier way to find out what categories would be best for you to choose. Once again Publisher Rocket works very quickly to find the ABSR of the #1 and #10 books in any category. Below is a screenshot of Publisher Rocket in action. I wanted to find horror categories, so in the upper right box you can see that I typed 'horror'. Publisher Rocket went out to Amazon, found all the categories associated with that word, and listed them out for me with the requirements to rank #1 and #10 in each of the categories it found.

By clicking on the 'check it out' link to the right of each category, Publisher Rocket will take you directly to that category's rank listing of books. As you can see, I would need to sell at least 34 books a day to rank #1 in all these categories. What I do is copy and paste these screens into Excel where I can sort them by their rankings and find categories to put my book into that will give it a good chance of achieving the 'Amazon Best Seller' status flag.

Step 6 – Advertising

If you've made it this far with me, it's because you are serious about marketing your books and getting the word out to potential readers. In order to do this effectively, you are going to, at some point, have to purchase advertising.

In the book launches I have designed for my clients, the advertising is an indispensable component. Without getting your book in front of potential readers, you will not be successful in marketing.

Before getting into details, there are a few terms you should be familiar with.

Clicks vs Impressions – In online advertising, there are different ways of charging for ads. Some advertisers might just charge a one-time fee. A popular way you will be charged is either by the number of 'clicks' your ad generates or the number of 'impressions' your ad is given.

Impressions – This term simply refers to the number of times your advertiser shows your book's ad to potential buyers. Generally, advertisers charge by the 1,000 impressions. The advantage of using impressions is not always apparent and depends on how your advertiser goes about deciding who's ad gets shown. Generally, most advertisers use a bidding process. All the ads for a particular type of keyword or targeted product are considered by their bid, and often the winning bid gets the impression. However, it's often more complicated than that and if your advertiser is offering impressions as a way to charge you, be sure to understand how that advertiser makes these decisions.

Clicks – As the name implies, this charging method is used to pay for the ad every time a potential customer clicks on an ad. This might seem like the best method on the surface, but there are often a lot of things going on that could favor you paying for impressions rather than clicks. Placement, bidding, and history could come into play. The most important factor being how the advertising company decides to show your ad.

CTR – This stands for Click Through Rate and is the measure of the number of 'clicks' an ad gets per the number of impressions served. So if your ad is shown 1,000 times and ten people click on the ad, that's a 1% CTR. This measurement is most important when you are paying for impressions. It stands to reason that you are getting more for your money if 100 people click on your ad rather than only 10 people.

BID - The amount of money you are willing to pay for a particular ad. When an ad spot is available and it's attached to something you have indicated as being a place you want to show your ad, then your ad is put into a bidding process. This 'something' could be a targeted author's following, such as a fan of Stephen King receives an email from the advertiser and several new books this fan might enjoy are presented. There will be a limited number of books the advertiser will show to this fan, so as not to be overwhelming. The highest bids for one of these spots will have their ads shown.

SEARCH PAGE – This is a sales page generated when a customer enters a keyword phrase in the search box. The search engine calculates what will be most relevant and most likely to result in a buy to the keyword phrase entered, creates a page of those items ranked from #1 to the bottom of the page, and shows it to you.

PRODUCT PAGE – This is the page generated by your online store. It will show relevant information about the product, the price, any discounts, product reviews, ads for related products, and a way to purchase the product.

When I do a book launch, there are specific advertisers I use. These advertisers fall into two categories: 'Launch Only' and 'Ongoing'.

Launch Only advertisers are a onetime deal. There are three of these I use to help launch a client's book to Amazon Best Seller status.

1. BKnights – This service has been around for a while and only charges $5 for the service. (there are upgrades available). Your book has to be discounted in order for your ad to be accepted. BKnights has over 50,000 email subscribers and several thousand website visitors per day. Apply at https://www.fiverr.com/share/4zzweb BKnights is a great way to push sales on a book launch. Because they require your book to be discounted, it's not feasible for an ongoing advertising platform. I've used this service and while you can't concretely define how many sales their ads result in, It's fair to say there is an increase in sales

when your ad runs with them. After a book launch, and a substantial amount of time has passed with your book being full priced, you can always discount again and run another promotion.

2. BookSends – You will be charged $40 for non-fiction, between $20 - $60 for adult fiction, and $10 for children's books. BookSends requires the following: At least 5 reviews with a high average rating, Sales price less than $3 and at least 50% off full price, Lowest price the book has been in the past 90 days. The number of subscribers and pricing depends on your discount and the genre. Apply here - https://booksends.com/advertise.php Again, BookSends is not feasible for ongoing advertising because they require you to discount your book. Always keep it in mind when you want to run a promotion however.

3. BuckBooks – The Kindle book must be 99 cents. You must have at least 10 reviews with an average 3.8 stars. Pricing is $9 for fiction, $29 for non-fiction. BuckBooks is

the brain child of author Matt Stone and his friend Rob Archangel. He is convinced that promoting your new release at $.99 is the best way to get sales generating for your book. Because of the price restriction, Buckbooks is launch only advertising. Apply here - http://buckbooks.net/promotions/

Ongoing Advertising
There are two main advertising platforms I use to launch clients' books to Amazon Best Seller status over the five-day launch period and beyond. BookBub and Amazon Advertising. These two are the main powerhouses in book advertising today but there are others including The Fussy Librarian, Onlinebookclub.org, Goodreads.com and more. I'm just going to go over the two main ones I use. See the end of this book to contact me for more information.

Amazon Advertising

The Amazon ad interface is not easy to learn and use. Once you do get the hang of it, it can cost you a lot of money. However, many experts feel that simply using their advertising services gives your book a boost in whether Amazon will put your book in front of potential readers. I think it's safe to say an investment of $35 to $100 a week will be worth the expense to train the Amazon algorithm to show your book.

Once you have signed into the Amazon Advertising console https://amazon.advertising.com, if you wish you can create a portfolio. This is a folder to hold ads of the same type. I use them to group ads for a particular book, or series. It's just a way to organize your ads.

When you are ready to create a new advertising campaign click the button that says 'Create Campaign'. You will be taken to a screen offering you three choices.

Sponsored Products – This is the structure I use the most. It lets you advertise one of your books.

Sponsored Brands – You can use this if you have at least three books to advertise.

Lockscreen Ads – These ads show up on Kindle Readers and Fire Tablets when they are in idle mode. I have used these successfully by invoking a famous author for instance for my horror story I used ad text that invoked Stephen King.
Choose "Sponsored Products" by clicking the 'Continue' button under that heading.

Campaign Name – I usually name my ads by the book name, the date(s) and what type of campaign it is (keyword or book targeted).
You can assign the ad to a portfolio if you have created one. Give your campaign a start and end date (you can leave the end date blank if you just want to run the ad continuously). Give the ad a daily budget.

Take what you can afford to spend on Amazon Ads per week, divide that by two (because we are going to set up both keyword and book target ads), and divide that by seven. You can always change your budget, so don't get too hung up on it here.

Targeting – You can have Amazon automatically set up keywords or books to target but I don't recommend it. Choose 'Manual Targeting' here. Amazon uses some sort of funky algorithm to assign keywords generated from your title and book description. They are rarely useful.

Campaign Bidding Strategy - There are three options here, I always choose the middle one but let me give a little explanation here. Amazon wants to maximize sales. Every time you sell a book, Amazon makes money, so it stands to reason they are going to show the ads that are most likely to make them money. The algorithm is designed to learn when a particular ad is likely to result in a purchase. Using this information, it can decide to raise or lower your bid depending on which strategy you choose.

Dynamic Bids – Down Only - When a keyword you have assigned to this ad, or a book is about to be used to put together a page to show the Amazon Customer, Amazon checks all products that have attached themselves to that keyword phrase or book. It then goes through a process to decide which product is placed at the top, placed on the page at all, or not chosen. Competition depends on how many products (books) have chosen this keyword or book. There are a lot of factors involved, but the one we are concerned with here is the **Bidding Strategy**. Selecting Dynamic Bids – Down Only will make Amazon lower your bid if it thinks this particular spot is likely not to result in a sale. If you have experience running ads, you might want to choose this option to save money, but I wouldn't choose it the first time out.

Dynamic Bids – Up and Down – Amazon will raise or lower your bid based on what the algorithm thinks your ad's chances of resulting in a sale are. If it seems unlikely, Amazon will lower your bid. If it seems like it will result in a sale, it will raise your bid by a maximum of 100%.

Fixed Bids – The algorithm will always use your default bid no matter what it thinks your chances are.

Adjust Bids by Placement – I wouldn't recommend using this at first but if you find you are not seeing any spending (meaning your ads are not being shown) you can adjust this, so your bid is increased by a certain percentage to increase the chances of your ad being shown. You can do this for 'Top of Search' meaning you are bidding to have your ad placed above the top of a search page generated by a keyword phrase you have attached to this ad. You can also put in adjustments for bidding on placement on 'product pages', giving your ad an increased chance of showing up on a targeted book's sales page.

For first time ads, I choose 'Dynamic Bids – Up and Down' and no adjustments. If you are seeing a lot of clicks but few sales, one thing you can do is change this to 'Down Only' to reduce your expense. There are other, better ways to address this however and we'll talk about those. Again, if you are not seeing any impressions or clicks, you can increase your bid adjustment giving your ad a better chance of being selected.

'Ad Format' – There are two choices here, either select text you create to be shown with your ad (Custom Text ad) or just run the ad (Standard ad). If you advertising just one of your books, select the Custom Text and come up with ad copy. (write me if you want help with this). Choosing **Custom Text** will only let you advertise one book. If you select **Standard ad**, you will be able to advertise several of your books. This is handy if you want to advertise a series.

Products - Here, Amazon will show you a list of all the products you have available for sale. Choose the book you want to promote (or in the case of a Standard ad you can choose several).

Automatic Targeting – If you've chosen this option, you will need to set a default bid. Generally, the default starts at $.75 but there will be a suggested bid shown below the entry box. Use the suggested bid. You can always lower this later if you are getting for too many clicks that aren't giving you sales.

Negative Targeting – You can tell Amazon not to show your ad for certain keywords or targeted products. I wouldn't worry about this right now, after you've had some time go by and can look at the results of your campaigns, you may want to use this to keep certain keywords or products from triggering a showing that you know won't result in a sale.

Manual Targeting – This is the option I strongly suggest you use. You will be able to enter a list of keywords or ASIN's to target your ad to.

Suggested – Amazon will generate a list of keywords for you here. You can add all or select only the ones you think will work.

Enter List – This allows you to either type in keywords or paste them in from a spreadsheet.

Upload File – If you prefer, you can download an Excel template from here and enter keywords into it. I'm not sure why you would want to do this however, as it's easier just to paste the list into the 'Enter List' screen.

Match Type – You can choose how Amazon matches customer's keyword phrases to your selected keywords. '**Broad**' – This option will match all your words in the keyword phrase in any order and include any related words (such as plurals, variations in spelling, and related words). '**Phrase**' will match only when the keyword phrase is contained within the search phrase. (customer types 'red bear diaries' and you have a keyword target of 'red bear'. This will be a match.) '**Exact**' – means what it says, there will only be a match when the customer's typed in keyword phrase matches exactly to your target keyword phrase.

Generally, when first setting up a campaign I select 'Broad'. If you are enough of an expert to fine tune this, then you might want to select another match type.

Getting keywords and target books can be time consuming. You can find keywords by first clearing your browser history, then going to Amazon, selecting 'Kindle Store' for your search category, and type in a keyword you would associate with your book. Amazon will show you keywords that have been recently used that are similar to the one you typed in. Do this with as many keywords as you can think of, and then use some of the found keywords to find more.

To find books to target, find a book that you know readers who will like your book would purchase. Find that book on Amazon, and then scroll to 'Product Details' and record the ASIN number. Go to the section marked 'Products related to this item' and select the books there, record their ASIN's and then start with another book. Repeat the process as much as you can. Don't worry too much about duplicating as once you enter the ASIN's into the Books to target section of your ad, Amazon will remove any duplicates.

A quick and easy way to find keywords and books to target is to purchase Publisher Rocket. A tool that will do all this work for you in a few minutes plus more. You can also find some excellent teaching videos on Dave Chesson's site with valuable information on how to set up and run Amazon ads.

https://kindlepreneur.com/

As always, please consider telling me how I did with this teaching booklet. You can write to me at mj@mjalbertbooks.com.

BookBub Ads

Quite possibly the most powerful advertising tool you can use is BookBub. This service has millions of subscribers all over the world and a straightforward interface to set up and run ads to reach them.

Set up an author profile at BookBub, and then you can begin. (You should be aware that claiming your author profile could take up to a week). Once it is set up, you can add your books to your profile. This isn't a requirement to run ads, but it does make parts of it easier.

Bookbub artwork – When you create a BookBub ad, you will need a 300 x 250 pixel jpg file. I suggest you sign up for the BookBub mailing list so you can see this type of artwork. You can create your own, hire an artist to do it for you, or use BookBub's interface to create one. While the artwork is important, if you use the Bookbub interface and you aren't getting a lot of traction with the ads, you should consider designing your own or hiring someone to do it for you.

1. **Designing your own** – This is fairly easy if you are familiar at all with Microsoft Paint or another image creation software. Simply create a 300 x 250 pixel jpg file,

copy your bookcover's jpg and reduce it in size to about 150 x 250 pixels. Copy that into your new blank file, use the eyedropper to select one of the colors from your book cover and then use the bucket to paste that color into the rest of the file. Create a text box and make sure you use a font color that will contrast nicely with the background, then type in your sales pitch. Below that use a button, I usually color them red, and paste that below your sales pitch and add a blurb like 'BUY NOW', 'ON SALE', 'ONLY 99 CENTS'. That's it. You're ad art is ready to go. Try different background colors, buttons or no buttons, and different sales pitches. I create five to ten different ads when I do a launch.

2. **Hiring an expert** – Anyone who designs book covers can design a bookbub ad for you. In fact, when you get your cover done you should ask if they can create a bookbub ad. The best place I've found is on fiverr.com. Simply search for bookbub and you'll have a lot of artists to preview and choose from.

3. **Using the interface** – I have tried this and not had a lot of luck getting traffic with it. The ad looks like what it is: a computer-

generated image. I see a lot of authors using it though, so I think it must work to some extent. If you can't afford to hire someone (and honestly, Fiverr artists are very cheap) and you aren't proficient enough with image creation, then try it. If it doesn't work, try changing the design and sales pitch.

Bookbub Targeting: When you set up a bookbub ad, you have the option to target categories and authors. You want to do this because if you set your parameters too broad you aren't going to get much traffic. Bookbub needs to know which customers to target and choosing categories is easy to decide, and it will narrow the focus somewhat, but you will also want to find authors who write books your readers enjoy reading.

    The obvious thing would seem to be to target a successful, famous author who writes in your genre. Unfortunately, this doesn't work. The followers of famous authors rarely want to step outside their favorite writer's sphere. What will happen is you will get very few clicks on your ad. I have seen it work (in particular I once targeted Nora Roberts for a client who wrote a romance and it seemed to work) but it rarely lasts more than a day. After that, you are showing the ad to people who simply don't care about 'lesser' authors. You want to find authors who have followings between 10,000 and 100,000. These authors are well known but not so famous that their following is too broad.

Go to Amazon and look up a book similar to yours (or use one of your books if you are already published). Look at the 'Also bought' section and note down the authors there. Go back to your Bookbub ad design and click on 'Add Authors' and then search for each of the authors you found. Note down the number of followers they have and use the ones who have a following in the above range. You now should see the needle has moved to the green. If not check your categories and your author again.

One thing I've started doing that seems to work really well is to target several authors with small followings, adding them in as targets until I have enough to make the needle go into the green.

Schedule – You can run this ad continuously or set a date range for it.

There is no right or wrong here and it's mostly personal preference. You will need to be checking on how your ad is doing on a daily basis either way.

Total Campaign Budget: The ad will stop showing when the budget has been spent. You can always come back and edit the ad, to increase the budget if you want. Set it based on how you are budgeting your ad campaign. You can set a daily budget and come back each day to increase it. (not recommended because you are going to miss some hours of the day most likely. Your ad will stop when the budget runs out and won't start again until you increase it). You can set the budget for the entire campaign if you wish.

Pacing – You can set the budget to spend as quickly as possible or spread it out over your scheduled run. If you are going to check and possibly increase the budget daily, then set it to 'spend as quickly as possible'. If you want to set the budget for the entire campaign I suggest you use the 'spead it out' option.

Bid – You can buy ad space based on clicks or impressions.

CPM – Bid for ad space paying for 1,000 impressions

CPC - Bid for ad space based on the number of times a customer clicks your ad

Here again, it would seem to be a no brainer. Why pay to show your ad to people when you can pay only when they click on it? Here's the thing: BookBub is going to show your ad when it thinks it will be profitable. Using CPC will work for a while but over time you will see less and less placements meaning you are going to get fewer clicks. The best Bid type to use is CPM and then make sure you are monitoring the ad. If your CTR (click through rate) is low, pause that ad, copy it and make changes to the artwork, sales pitch, and/or author targets.

Naming your ad – You will be creating and running several ads and you want to be able to quickly identify what type of ad you are looking at. I use a naming convention that starts with the targeted author(s) name(s), the background color used, and a few words of the sales blurb to identify the ad.

Monitoring your ads – If an ad isn't working there are several reasons that could be affecting it.

1. Your sales pitch isn't right. Make sure it sizzles and makes the customer curious enough to click on the ad.

2. The artwork isn't eye catching. This can happen and the only thing you can do is try to make sure you have several different images to work with.

3. The target authors aren't working for you. Another reason to design several ads is to choose several different authors to target. Some authors will start out great for you, then you might find they taper off. Usually this only happens with CPC bidding, but it can happen with CPM as well. All you can do is turn the ad off and choose one with a different author. You can always try it again a month or two later on.

Overall, Bookbub ads are very powerful but they will also probably be the most expensive ones you run. To make them profitable you will need to monitor them daily and adjust according to what is going on with your click through rate. There are several classes out there on how to be successful with Bookbub ads. A good place to start is Dave Chesson or search on Youtube for David Gaughran.

One final piece of advice. If you aren't getting any clicks, then change your ad. If you are getting clicks, but no sales you need to take a close at your book's cover and description. If your description doesn't really sizzle, you won't sell books. Use your 'street team' of early readers to give you feedback on the book descriptions you come up with and try using the more popular ones.

Armed with this knowledge you should be able to successfully run your own book launch now! Just know that this is the start. To make your writing profitable you need to continue learning all you can about marketing, genre, and reaching out to your audience. For more information, please drop me an email at mj@mjalbertbooks.com.

Here is hoping you find a new career in the independent book publishing world!

Additional Advertising venues

Here are a few more places you can advertise books. Many of these have free campaigns you can put your book in. The reason they don't charge you is that they make money as Amazon Affiliates. If someone buys your book, Amazon pays the affiliate a percentage of that sale.

Many of these sites require that you discount your book. There are some that have free programs as well as upgrades to the advertising for which you must pay for.

Go to my website where you can find updates as I revisit the list and remake it.

M.J. Albert Books

30 Sites offering free advertising

Robin Reads – 194,000 members. Several options available both free and paid.

https://robinreads.com/genre-divide/

Book Reader Magazine - Free to submit. $20 to guarantee a featured spot on the homepage for 7 days. 18,400 Twitter followers, 1,300 Facebook fans. Part of the Author Ad Network

https://bookreadermagazine.com/submit-your-book/

Book Goodies Kids - Kids books up to Teen and YA. Can submit your book for placement for free. Paid options range from $49 up to $229. Part of Author Ad Network.

http://bookgoodieskids.com/

Awesome Gang - You can submit your book and get a page on their site for free. Paying the optional $10 gives your book priority homepage listing for 2 days plus email and social blast to 53,000 Facebook fans, and 15,700 Twitter followers. Part of the Author Ad Network.

https://awesomegang.com/submit-your-book/

Pretty-hot.com : The site does have a free option, but the form also has an option for a paid listing for $25 to get a featured listing for 7 days plus email and social blast. 6,350 facebook fans, 12,000 Twitter fans. Also part of the Author Ad network of book promotion sites you can purchase a package for through them. 150,000 Facebook followers, 200,000 Twitter Followers, 10,000 other Social, 20,000 email subscribers

https://pretty-hot.com/submit-your-book/

Digital Book Today – To qualify for a free listing the book must be available for free 'for a minimum of 24 hours', **Fiction**: 100+ pages, 4.0 + stars, 18+ reviews. **Non-Fiction less than 100 pages** 60+ reviews, 4.2 + stars. **Non-fiction 100+ pages** 40+ reviews, 4.0+ stars. **Children's books** 125+ reviews, 4.0+ stars. 'Featured Free Book' promotion available for $20(current price, will be going up to $30 in the future), no minimum requirements.

https://digitalbooktoday.com/join-our-team/12-top-100-submit-your-free-book-to-be-included-on-this-list/

EReader Love - Will advertise free ebooks to over 2000 readers. Paid options available, but these were sold out at the time of this writing.

http://www.ereaderlove.com/contact-us-submit-a-book/

Book Bongo - This service has over 500,000 people in facebook groups and email lists. No requirements but they suggest you discount your book during the promotion period. Several options available from free to $149.99. The last gives you a 30 to 60 second video and soundtrack which will be promoted and made available to you.

https://bookbongo.com/submit/

Discount Book Man – Free promotion, no requirements, Featured option for $15. No indication how many people are reached but the site looks professional.

https://discountbookman.com/book-promotion/

eBooks Habit ebook must be offered at $2.99 or less. Must have at least 5 reviews, no erotica accepted. Email and Twitter promotions. Over 485,000 followers. 3 tiers of advertising, Basic for free Guaranteed placement for $10 and extra tweets included for $15.

http://ebookshabit.com/for-authors/

Kindle Book Review – Kindle book must be free. Must have at least a 3.5 star rating at time of promotion. 4 options available; Free, $10, $15, and $20. Over 30,000 subscribers.

http://ebookshabit.com/for-authors/

<u>One Hundred Free Books</u> – <u>Free and paid ad options. Submit a request and they will contact you.</u>

https://ohfb.com/book-sale-notice/

ContentMo.com Ad options from free to $99.

21,000 twitter, 1,000,000 Facebook reader group, 7,000 email subscribers, 67,000 views/mo on Pinterest.

https://contentmo.com/submit-your-free-ebook-promo

Topless Cowboy – Romance books, hundreds of followers. Submit for free.

https://toplesscowboy.com/submit-your-book/

New Free Kindle Books - Free listing to 4,100 subscribers. About 10% get chosen. They have a gold and silver pay level but as of 05/17/2021 this service is 'temporarily offline'.

https://newfreekindlebooks.com/authors/

Frugal Tips and Freebies: No charge listing. "5.1 million views" - for free ebooks only. http://www.frugal-freebies.com/p/submit-freebie.html

Freebooks.com facebook page: free promotion to 2700 followers https://www.facebook.com/FreeBooksCommunity   Website: https://www.freebooks.com/

Book Angel UK: Free promotion but book must be available on Amazon UK and/or Kobo. Free or discounted. http://bookangel.co.uk/submit-a-book/

Armadillo Books: Free listing available on four different properties. https://armadilloebooks.com/contact/

DealseekingMom: Must be a 'deal'. Email your offer here: https://dealseekingmom.com/about/contact/

Ebook Corner Kafe : 138,000 followers on Facebook only. Read instructions and 'like' the facebook page Ebook Corner Kafe facebook   Then follow the instructions in the comments.

Author's Den - Millions of readers. Must sign up for membership. Promotions are in the form of member benefits and run anywhere from Free to $800/year. https://www.authorsden.com/

ebookStage you must create an account. There are free promotions available as inclusion in a daily email. They have 5000 facebook followers, and almost that in twitter followers.

https://www.ebookstage.com/how-to-promote-your-ebook

ReadIndies – Facebook group with 18,000 members. Need to make a request to join to post your book. There is also an associated site readindies.blogspot.com where you can post as well.

Reading Deals: 2 plans, one is free but not guaranteed, book must be discounted. The other is $29 which guarantees your book to be featured. They have 35,000 subscribers. Reading Deals ads

Book Praiser: offers a free plan and two paid plans. Unknown number of subscribers.

https://bookpraiser.com/authorresourcesinfo/

Crave Freebies: for free kindle book promotion only. Contact at least 2 days before book is offered for free. There are paid options to guarantee exposure to 'thousands of readers'. Email: mailto:icravefreebies@gmail.com?subject=Review%20Service

All Authors site

Unknown number of subscribers. Must sign up to use their promotions. One is free the paid option is $59.

https://allauthor.com/pricing/

The Book Circle

'1,000's of interested readers.' Promotions are for discounted Kindle books and are free or up to $20.

https://www.book-circle.com/submit-free-kindle-ebook-listing/

Best Book Monkey

12,000 monthly website visitors and 13,000 subscribers to email list plus 60,000 social media followers.

Free promo and 'gold packages' starting around $10.

https://bestbookmonkey.com/promo-packages/

Paid Advertising Venues

Below is a list of sites that will promote your book for a fee.

Book Life - $149

They target book-sellers, librarians, agents, publishers, film producers and production companies.https://booklife.com/about-us/pw-select.html

Dango Books

5,000 subscribers $10 deals to promote your book

https://dangobooks.com/partners-overview/

Indies Today

'thousands of avid readers' Promotions costs depend on price of book, under $10 to $40.

https://indiestoday.com/book-promotion/

ReaderIQ: Prices and number of subscribers vary. Book must have at least 5 reviews, be the length of a novel, professional cover design, offered for free or discounted at least 50%.

https://www.ereaderiq.com/authors/submissions/dds/

The EReaderCafe: 6 different options priced from $25 to $40. 91k Facebook Fans, 58k Email Subscribers, 20k Pinterest Pinners, 3k Twitter followers.

https://theereadercafe.com/sell-more-books/

Lovely Books – for free kindle books, either promotion or permanent. Facebook, Twitter, and Email promotions. 40+ facebook group promotions available for $10.

http://lovelybookpromotions.com/submit-your-kindle-freebie/

Readers Hideaway - unknown number of followers. Paid ads only running from $20 to $199. Part of the Author Ad Network.

https://readershideaway.com/author-advertising/

Indie Author News – Must fill out a form to get advertising info.

https://www.indieauthornews.com/p/promote-my-book.html

Book Barbarian – 46,500 subscribers. SF and F books only. Must be stand alone or first in series. Must have a minimum of ten reviews. https://bookbarbarian.com/ad-pricing/

Supplements to Independent Author Marketing

Templates for contacting possible reviewers.

Subject: want to be on my street team?

Hi _____ (first name),

I've been talking about it forever, and now it's finally happening! _____

_____ (book title) is almost done, and I'm getting ready to launch it.

I'm putting together an inner-circle street team, and you're invited! You'll get a free copy of the book before it's even published, so you can be one of the first to read it. You'll also get a backstage pass to the launch. You'll get to see how I launch the book and how it works as it's all unfolding.

In return, I ask that you review the book by _____ (date you'll publish into stealth mode) and help spread the word when we launch.

What do you say? You in?

Either way, thanks for being part of the community. I appreciate you!

_____ (your first name)

Review request to a stranger

Subject: would you like a review copy of a
_____ (genre) book?

Hi _____ (first name or user
ID),

 I saw your review of
_____(similar book) on
Amazon, and I was wondering if you
might like an advance review copy of a
similar book. I've written a book called

_____
(title of your book). Like

_____
__(title of the book they reviewed), it's a

_____
_____

(describe your book, highlighting the
similarities to the other book they
reviewed).

I think you'd really enjoy this book
because _____

_____

_____

(why you think they might like it— tie in
to something from their review if possible)

Would you like a review copy in Kindle or
PDF? I'd be happy to send you either—
just let me know.

Thanks!

_____ (Your name)

Hi _____(first name),

How are you doing? Great, I hope!

_____
_____

(1-2 sentences referring to something
currently going on with them, wishing
them well, maybe offering to help with
something)

The other reason I'm writing is I'm
releasing a new book
soon,_____ (title of your
book), and I was wondering if you would
be interested in a (free) review copy? I
want to get a little bit of feedback on it
before I send it out into the world. I'd love
to hear what you think! Of course, you'd be
under no obligation to review it, but if you

like it, I'd be very grateful for a short testimonial.

Please let me know if you'd be willing to do this!

Thanks!

_____ (your name)

Hi _____ (name),

I've been a fan since

_____

(when you became a fan: the date or a
memorable thing that happened), and I

_____

_____

(why you admire them or some other
connection). I'm writing to you because
I'm about to release a new book,
_____ (title of your book).

I believe this book would be valuable and
interesting to you and your audience

because

_____

_____ (how it specifically relates
to their interests and/or stuff they talk
about on their platform).

I was wondering if you'd like an advance review copy. I'd be honored to have you read it.

Of course, you'd be under no obligation to review it, but if you like it, I'd be very grateful for a short testimonial. I'm planning to launch on _____ (launch date), so I'd need any feedback by _____ (three weeks before launch date).

Would you like a review copy in Kindle or PDF? I'd be happy to send you either— just let me know.

Thanks,

_____ (your name)

_____ (your website or "Author of the forthcoming book [title]")

Launch to Amazon Best Seller Status

Project Timeline

Week 1: Develop cover design. Decide on how you will design it or who you will hire to do it. Allow about 2 weeks (due in week 3) for finalizing the cover.

Week 2: Develop your book description and send it out to any early readers you have for their comments.

Week 3: Contact potential editorial reviewers and reader reviewers. Sign up for an email service such as Mailchimp, Mailerlite, or Convertkit. You are looking to get at least 40 names of people who will commit to doing a reader review and five to ten who will commit to an editorial review. If your manuscript is edited and ready for publishing, you can send them the pdf or epub version now. You should have your Cover and book description finalized.

Week 4: Decide which categories and keywords you will use. **Soft publish your book**. (Upload it through KDP into Amazon) Contact your early readers and committed reviewers to let them know the book is available and on sale for the next three weeks. Contact Booksend, BKnights, and Buckbooks to set up promotions.

Week 5: Finalize your Author platform. You should have a landing page, Amazon Author profile, Bookbub account, and a Goodreads account. Optional: social media accounts, website. Create or have created for you, a couple different Bookbub ads. You can start preparing your ads in Amazon and Bookbub.

Week 6: Launch on Tuesday.

Make sure your ads are running. Monitor progress, click rates, impressions, and sales. Adjust as needed. The launch will end on Saturday. Sunday morning you can price your book at your standard price.

Post Launch:

Decide on a budget, run Bookbub and Amazon ads, continue to monitor and make adjustments with your goal being to reach a point where your ads are paid for by your royalties. This could take awhile, be patient, keep adjusting and testing. Remember 60% of being an Independent Author is marketing!

The most important element for independent authors is

WRITE ANOTHER BOOK!

How to Price your book

One of the questions I always get is 'how much should I sell my book for?'

There is no hard rule here, but I suggest you research book prices for the type of book you have written and price accordingly.

If sales are off the chart, raise the price a little. If you aren't getting sales and you are confident your ads are working, lower the price a little.

I would suggest that about every three months or so, run another promotion.

Kindle Unlimited: To KU or not KU?

There are many voracious readers out there that have signed up for Amazon's Kindle Unlimited program. This allows them to choose any book in KU and read it. For authors, it means you can get your book out in front of millions of potential readers.

The tradeoff is that you can't sell your book on other venues like Barnes & Noble or Apple Books. You can only sell it on Amazon if you are enrolled in KU.

If you are a fiction writer and going to write multiple books, I suggest you enroll in KU. It's a three-month program and you can either pull the book out or make the decision to keep it in KU at the end of the term. You won't make as much per sale (In KU you get paid by the number of pages read) but you will reach a wider audience and potentially create a large fan base.

Some authors will put one book of a series in KU and leave the rest out, making buyers have to purchase the book in the normal fashion. If you want to 'go wide' and make your book available in other venues, then KU is not for you.

There is an argument for putting your book in KU and also a good one for not doing that. I suggest you try it for the three-month period. See if it works for you.

For more

The business of Independent Book Marketing is still growing, still changing. Keep up with what's going on by signing up at my site.

https://www.mjalbertbooks.com/contact-me.html

If you need help with your book description go here:

https://www.mjalbertbooks.com/blurb.html

Need a report on Categories and Keywords?

https://mjalbertbooks.com/key

Want to be part of a class and learn how to market your book with other authors? I teach a six to eight week class, one hour a week as we go through each of the six elements and then launch our books with a five day promo blitz aimed at achieving Amazon Best Seller status. Contact me below to find out when the next class is and pricing.

https://www.mjalbertbooks.com/bestsellergroups.html

I'd really love to hear from you what you thought of my book. What helped, what was not clear, what you would like to know more about. You can contact me at https://www.mjalbertbooks.com/about.html#/

Printed in Great Britain
by Amazon